Yukonstyle

SARAH BERTHIAUME

yukonstyle

translated by
Nadine Desrochers

Playwrights Canada Press
Toronto

Yukonstyle © 2014 by Sarah Berthiaume
English translation © 2014 by Nadine Desrochers
Originally published in French by Éditions Théâtrales in 2013

For professional or amateur production rights, please contact the publisher.

LIBRARY AND ARCHIVES CANADA CATALOGUING IN PUBLICATION
Berthiaume, Sarah, 1983-

[Yukonstyle. English]

   Yukonstyle / Sarah Berthiaume ; translated by Nadine Desrochers.

Translation of French play with same title.
Issued in print and electronic formats.
ISBN 978-1-77091-269-4 (pbk.).--ISBN 978-1-77091-270-0 (pdf).--
ISBN 978-1-77091-271-7 (epub)

   I. Desrochers, Nadine, translator II. Title. III. Title: Yukonstyle.
English

PS8603.E76373Y8313 2014   C842'.6   C2014-904106-3
                                                  C2014-904107-1

We acknowledge the financial support of the Canada Council for the
Arts, the Ontario Arts Council (OAC), the Ontario Media Development
Corporation, and the Government of Canada through the Canada Book
Fund for our publishing activities.

 Canada Council
for the Arts
Conseil des arts
du Canada

 ONTARIO ARTS COUNCIL
CONSEIL DES ARTS DE L'ONTARIO
an Ontario government agency
un organisme du gouvernement de l'Ontario

 Canadä

 Ontario
Ontario Media Development
Corporation

This play is dedicated to Christian and Mitsue,
my favourite Yukoners.

Yukonstyle was first produced in French in Paris, France, at La Colline—théâtre national between March 28 and April 27, 2013, and toured in May and December 2013. It was co-produced by Compagnie Voyages d'Hiver; La Colline—théâtre national, Paris; Théâtre Vidy-Lausanne; and Centre dramatique national des Alpes, Grenoble. It received support from MC2: Grenoble, the Consulat général de France à Québec, and the Délégation générale du Québec à Paris, as well as artistic participation from the Jeune Théâtre national. The production featured the following cast and creative team:

Garin: Dan Artus
Kate: Flore Babled
Dad: Jean-Louis Coulloc'h
Yuko: Cathy Ming Jung

Director: Célie Pauthe
Artistic collaboration: Denis Loubaton
Set design: Guillaume Delaveau, assisted by Tomoyo Funabachi
Lighting design: Joël Hourbeigt
Costume design: Marie La Rocca
Sound design: Aline Loustalot
Images: Guillaume Delaveau, asssisted by François Weber
Choreography constultant: Thierry Thieû Niang

The play was first produced in Canada by Théâtre d'Aujourd'hui in Montreal between April 9 and May 4, 2013. The production featured the following cast and creative team:

Kate: Sophie Desmarais
Garin: Vincent Fafard
Dad: Gérald Gagnon
Yuko: Cynthia Wu-Maheux

Director: Martin Faucher
Assistant director: Emanuelle Kirouac-Sanche
Set design: Max-Otto Fauteux
Costume design: Denis Lavoie
Lighting design: Etienne Boucher
Music and sound design: Alexander MacSween
Makeup and hair: Angelo Barsetti

The English version of *Yukonstyle* was commissioned by the Canadian Stage Company and made possible thanks to the support of the Canada Council for the Arts in the form of the Translation of Canadian Theatre Works program. The play was produced by the Canadian Stage Company in association with Hopscotch Collective and the Theatre Department, Faculty of Fine Arts, York University. The English-language translation premiered at the Berkeley Street Theatre in Toronto on October 13, 2013, and featured the following cast and creative team:

Kate: Kate Corbett
Garin: Ryan Cunningham
Pops: François Klanfer

Yuko: Grace Lynn Kung

Director: Ted Witzel
Set and costume design: Gillian Gallow
Lighting design: Bonnie Beecher
Music composition and sound design: Richard Feren
Stage manager: Marcie Januska
Assistant stage manager: Maureen Callaghan

Canadian Stage also hosted a development workshop, with support from the Brian Linehan Charitable Foundation, in December 2012. For this workshop, the roles of Garin and Pops were performed by Meegwun Fairbrother and Quincy Armorer, respectively.

This play was written, in part, at a writers' colony held in Charlevoix, Quebec, by the Centre des auteurs dramatiques (CEAD) in the spring of 2009; this organization further supported the development of the play through a workshop in February and March of 2010.

CHARACTERS

Garin: Metis. Son of Pops and Goldie. Yuko's roommate.

Yuko: Japanese, living in exile in the Yukon. Garin's roommate.

Pops: Garin's father.

Goldie (played by the same actor as Yuko): Garin's mother. Yukon First Nations woman. Disappeared in the 1980s.

Kate: Young woman dressed Harajuku style, travelling across Canada by bus.

Jamie (played by the same actor as Garin): Saskatchewanian from Swift Current.

SET

A couch, at least.

OVERTURE

GARIN and YUKO are sitting on the couch. Perhaps one of them is holding a guitar. They sing "Steak for Chicken" by the Moldy Peaches.

SCENE 1: GREYHOUND

A road at night. KATE *is hitchhiking in her hardcore Lolita dress.*

GARIN
Whitehorse. Night. Winter.
Minus forty-five degrees Celsius. The threshold between cold and death.
A girl dressed like a doll is hitchhiking along the main drag.
Could be mistaken for a hooker, with her seventeen-year-old legs crammed in all that lace and her stubborn resolve to find herself on the road at this time of night.
Not a hooker, though.
Just a girl dressed like a doll at minus forty-five degrees Celsius.
She's cold.
Obviously.
Snow crunching under her platform boots.
Lace rustling on her frozen thighs.
A name makes its way from the warmth of her belly to the edge of her lips and escapes as a fine pink dew into the sharp Yukon night.
Jamie.
The girl sighs.

Shouldn't have gotten off.

Should've stayed on the bus one more night. Climb higher still. Get lost even deeper in the improbable North. Push this insane flight even further into the mountains, the fumes, the bison herds, and the A&Ws.

But.

Whitehorse.

The blurry image of a white stallion on streets paved with gold. So here she is.

Hitchhiking at minus forty-five degrees Celsius in her dolly outfit, standing on the threshold between cold and death.

I don't know her yet, this girl. But it shouldn't be long.

> *The sound of an engine. A horn.* KATE *takes her backpack and exits.*

She's arriving at my place.

SCENE 2: THE HITCHHIKING DOLL

> GARIN *is watching TV: a news report on the Robert Pickton trial is starting.* YUKO *enters, followed by* KATE. *They take their boots off.*

KATE
Bathroom?

> GARIN *turns, looks at them.*

YUKO
(indicating a door) Over there.

    KATE, still wearing her coat, disappears into the bathroom.

GARIN
Who's that?

YUKO
A girl. Hitchhiking.

GARIN
You know her?

YUKO
No.

GARIN
Why'd you pick her up?

YUKO
'Cause. Couldn't leave her there.

    Pause.

GARIN
She pees and goes.

YUKO
I don't want her to leave by herself.

GARIN

Well she's not sleeping here.

YUKO

She won't be any trouble, she'll just /

    KATE comes out of the bathroom, her coat over her arm.

KATE

The toilet won't flush.

    Pause. GARIN turns to face the TV. YUKO turns the volume way
    up, leans towards GARIN, and speaks to him in whispers.

YUKO

Garin, for fuck's sake /

GARIN

She's not sleeping here.

YUKO

I'm not asking you to sleep with her, I'm just asking you to /

GARIN

No.

YUKO

She'll sleep on the couch! It won't kill you to let her sleep on the
couch!

GARIN

I just don't want her to.

YUKO

Why not?

GARIN

For starters, it pisses me off that you bring someone into the house, so if on top of that she's a hooker, I /

YUKO

Oh, enough with the hooker thing!

GARIN

Look at how she's dressed!

YUKO

Precisely! If we let her go out like that, she'll just get assaulted by a gang of fucking N . . .

Pause.

GARIN

Natives. Say it. She'll just get assaulted by a gang of fucking Natives.

YUKO

By a gang of fucking Natives. Exactly.

GARIN

Too bad. Would serve her right for dressing like that.

YUKO

It's a look, a style. From Japan.

GARIN

You're all hookers and we're all rapists. That's just fucking great.

YUKO

Well too fucking bad, it's my couch.

She grabs the coat from KATE's hands and hangs it up.

(to KATE) Are you hungry?

GARIN gets up abruptly and exits to his room.

YUKO

Garin, my roommate. He never gets laid. Makes him nervous.

She hands KATE a pack of beef jerky.

KATE

(eating) Are you an Indian?

YUKO

I'm Japanese.

KATE

What are you doing here?

YUKO

I was fed up with Japan. I emigrated.

KATE

Sure, but why here?

YUKO

I searched the Web for the place in the world with the fewest Japanese people. It was here. So I sold everything and came over.

   Pause.

KATE

Damn.

YUKO

So you've heard of Harajuku, right?

KATE

No. What is it?

YUKO

A neighbourhood in Tokyo.

KATE

And why would I have heard of it?

YUKO

It's how you're dressed. Harajuku girl. That's what it's called. Your style.

KATE

I dress like this because I feel like it.

Pause.

YUKO

Look, it's not really any of my business, but if I were you, I'd make sure I feel like wearing something else when I'm hitchhiking at midnight in downtown Whitehorse.

KATE

Why?

YUKO

First, because you'll freeze your ass off, and second, because you're asking to be grabbed by people you don't necessarily want grabbing you.

KATE

I don't care. I'm already pregnant. Is there a clinic around here?

YUKO

What for?

KATE

An abortion. I'm seventeen.

Pause.

YUKO
Who's the father?

KATE
This guy from the bus.

YUKO
You slept with a guy from the bus?

KATE
I felt like it.

Pause.

Can I have a T-shirt? My dress itches when I sleep in it.

KATE settles in on the couch.

YUKO
As I look for something to clothe Kate's body,
cotton to put on her numb skin and inhabited belly,
Garin watches her breathe through his shut door.
One might imagine that he wants her
staring at her like that
from behind the plywood
listening to her body invade the living room
sensing her sickly sweet breath
beef-jerky-unborn-child

seep into the walls and the cracks of the couch.

But Garin doesn't want her.

No.

He's focused on painstakingly hating her

the stranger

the parasite

the lace-clad hooker

I've taken under my wing

and into my truck in the lower depths of the night.

If he didn't love me so much, Garin would throw Kate out without a second thought.

But.

Garin loves me, though of his love I am yet unaware.

So he retreats

and leaves her there

that girl

lets her sprawl her icy body into the cracks of the couch

and fall asleep.

Outside

a raven the size of a wolf

comes and sets his black feet on the windowsill.

It watches Garin go to bed

fully dressed,

folding his knees into his belly, like when he was two years old.

Garin falls asleep

and the raven smiles.

SCENE 3: WATCH OUT FOR NATIVES

Morning. GARIN *is standing by the couch, drinking coffee. He's watching* KATE. *She wakes up.*

KATE
Hey.

GARIN *turns away.*

Where's the girl?

GARIN
She's working.

Pause.

KATE
Don't you work too?

GARIN
Yes.

KATE
What do you do?

GARIN
I wash dishes.

KATE
Do you like it?

Pause.

GARIN
Do you like it?

KATE
What?

GARIN
Washing dishes.

KATE
No.

GARIN
So what makes you think I would like it?

KATE
I don't know. I was just asking.

Pause.

What's that girl's name again?

GARIN
Yuko.

KATE

Do you think she looks like an Indian?

GARIN

She's Japanese.

KATE

I know, but I think she looks like an Indian. Like, if she had braids, you could totally think she was an Indian.

Pause.

Are there a lot of Indians around here?

GARIN

More than you'd think.

KATE

I met this guy on the bus who said that you could always find them panhandling in groups in front of liquor stores because they don't have jobs. Apparently, no one wants to hire them because Indians just can't be trusted. It's in their culture, that they can't be trusted. The guy was saying that he had lived on a reserve for this contract he had, some construction job or whatever. Every month, when the government cheques would come in, there'd be this crazy massive beer bash all over the reserve. And I mean massive, real low-class shit. Apparently the men got so wasted that they had to lock up the women and children inside their houses. One year, they realized that the government cheques were on the same day as Hallowe'en. They had this big meeting to figure out what to do. So that nothing would happen to all the kids on the streets in their costumes, you know? So they decided to cancel Hallowe'en that year. That's what they decided. To cancel Hallowe'en. Pretty crazy, huh?

GARIN puts his cup on the floor.

You leaving?

GARIN
Yes.

KATE
Going to work?

GARIN
Yes.

He puts on his coat and boots.

KATE
Okay, bye.

KATE picks up GARIN's coffee and takes a sip. He comes back towards her and brutally grabs the mug from her hand.

KATE
Shit!

GARIN

That's the thing with us Indians. We just can't be trusted.

He leaves.

SCENE 4: THE HIGH COUNTRY INN

The kitchen in the High Country Inn. YUKO is cooking. GARIN is busy with the dishwasher.

KATE

Lunch in the kitchen at the High Country Inn.
The rush.
Harrowing.
Merciless.
The rush will bring them to their knees, the newbies
the poorly trained
the over-sensitive
the rush will make them lock themselves in the bathroom,
yelling that they can't take it
that they were given too many tables
that they can't finish their shift and just want to go home.
In the epicentre of the chaos
in the eye of the storm of the harrowing rush
there she is
the queen
in her white jacket and her houndstooth pants
towering from her six-foot height and her moose-like frame

there she is.

Magnificent.

Oriental.

Regal.

Don't fuck with Yuko in the kitchen of the High Country Inn.

She's in charge.

She can yell.

She can juggle

the fried calamari

and the mixed green salad with raspberry vinaigrette.

She holds the key to

the hot chicken sauce

the ham sushi

and the animal nuggets on the kids' menu.

She controls all.

She beholds all.

She triumphs, always.

On the other side of the kitchen,

stuck between the sink and the freezer,

is Garin

in his old Canucks T-shirt and his dirty apron

Garin, sweating

silent

piling dishes into the dishwasher's belly.

He doesn't flinch.

He's dreaming.

A name makes its way from the cold of his belly to the edge of his lips and escapes as a fine blue dew into the steam of the clean dishes.

Yuko.

And as though she might have heard him,
Yuko lifts her glance from the cutting board
and joins him in the tropical microclimate
of his oozing dishwasher.

YUKO
Where were you?

GARIN
Nowhere.

YUKO
The bosses were looking for you.

GARIN
How come?

YUKO
'Cause you're late. Again.

GARIN
No.

YUKO
Yes.

GARIN
No!

    YUKO sighs.

YUKO

You've got to stop doing that, Garin.

GARIN

Doing what?

YUKO

Spacing out. Disappearing. Flipping into Indian time when something's bothering you.

    Pause.

I told the bosses I had sent you to buy something.

GARIN

Thanks.

YUKO

I'm sick of covering for you. Buy a goddamn watch.

    Pause.

Was the girl still there when you got up?

GARIN

Yeah.

YUKO

I told her she could stay as long as she wants.

She heads towards her station.

GARIN
So, like, are you . . . are you? . . .

YUKO
Am I what?

GARIN
Well, I mean, do you want to . . . do her?

YUKO
The girl?

GARIN
Yeah.

YUKO
You're crazy.

GARIN
I don't know.

Pause.

YUKO
You think I'm into girls?

GARIN
How should I know?

YUKO
Is this because they told you I slept with Sandy or /

GARIN
You slept with Sandy?

YUKO
Well, I mean, not slept-slept, but /

GARIN
When?

>   *YUKO sighs.*

YUKO
(softly) After the conference, that time. We'd been drinking and she wanted to show me her new boobs, and . . . that's it. I went home with her. But the bosses can't find out, because /

GARIN
No, no. I get it.

>   *Pause.*

YUKO
What's wrong?

GARIN
Nothing.

YUKO

Why are you looking at me like that?

GARIN

Nothing, it's just . . .

YUKO

Just what?

GARIN

Just nothing. Just, you know. Cliché. The Japanese girl who ends up sleeping with the chick with the fake tits. It's classic.

YUKO

It's classic?

GARIN

Yeah, you know, like online porn.

Pause.

YUKO

I never should have told you.

She heads towards her station.

GARIN

You're so beautiful.

YUKO
What?

GARIN
Nothing. Sorry.

　　YUKO gets back to work.

KATE
And Garin clenches his fists
and starts his dishwasher.
But the ambient sound,
the muffled rumble that's causing the dishes to rattle slightly on
the counters,
that's not the dishwasher.
That's him.

SCENE 5: NICE OF YOU TO DROP BY

　　*POPS is home. He's listening to "Heart of Gold" by Neil Young,
　　which is booming from a radio. There's a knock at the door.*

POPS
(very loudly) Come in, Son!

　　GARIN comes in. POPS turns the radio off.

GARIN

Hey.

POPS

Hey, Son. Sorry about the mess.

GARIN

It's fine. What were you doing?

POPS

Just relaxing, taking it easy.

>   *Pause.*

Toi, ça va?

GARIN

I'm fine.

POPS

La job?

GARIN

Job is fine.

POPS

Fatigué?

GARIN

I'll get time off soon.

POPS

Now that's what I like to hear. *(indicating his glass)* En veux-tu?

GARIN

Sure.

> POPS *pours* GARIN *a drink, hands it to him. They drink.*

POPS

Still with that Chinese girl?

GARIN

Yes.

POPS

Elle va bien?

GARIN

She's fine.

> *Pause.*

POPS

Pis à part de ça?

GARIN

Nothing much.

> *Pause.*

POPS

Is it really cold out? I haven't been out today.

GARIN

It's like minus fifty.

POPS

Tabarnak . . .

Pause.

GARIN

I've got your cheque.

He takes a cheque out of his pocket, hands it to POPS.

POPS

(taking the cheque) Thanks, Son. Te souviens-tu du voisin?

GARIN

What neighbour?

POPS

The one with the dogs.

GARIN

No.

POPS

You don't remember him?

GARIN

No.

POPS

You know, he had dogs and lived in the building.

GARIN

I don't know.

POPS

En tout cas. He died.

GARIN

How?

POPS

He was eaten by his dogs. If you're hungry, we could order something.

GARIN

It's okay, Pops. I had food at work.

A long pause.

Watched TV recently?

POPS

I can't get any channels here.

GARIN

His trial has started.

POPS

Au gars qui . . .

GARIN

Robert Pickton. Yes. They're starting with six murders. Then
they'll do the other ones.

POPS

Okay. So they're doing them in batches.

GARIN

It's less complicated in terms of evidence.

POPS

Ben oui. Je comprends.

   Pause.

GARIN

Some of the disappearances date back to the eighties.

POPS

Ah oui.

GARIN

They found bodies they can't identify.

POPS

Hé ben.

GARIN

All Natives.

POPS

Hum.

GARIN

I think it's possible she might be one of them.

POPS

Qui ça?

GARIN

Her.

    Pause.

She was a hooker, right?

POPS

Hein?

GARIN

You can tell me, I'm not five anymore.

POPS

Why do you say that?

GARIN

Fuck, Pops. The women who vanish in the Low Track are usually not florists.

POPS

I really don't see where you're getting all this.

GARIN

Just tell me yes or no.

  Pause.

Is that how you met her? By paying her to sleep with you?

  POPS doesn't answer. GARIN gets up.

POPS

What are you doing, tu t'en vas?

GARIN

I'll come back when you're able to give me an answer.

POPS

Wait, Son, c'est pas /

GARIN

Good night.

  *GARIN leaves. POPS pours himself another gin. He turns the
  radio back on. Neil Young, very loud.*

SCENE 6: JAMIE'S HANDS

KATE is sitting on the couch. YUKO hands her a bowl and a glass of milk.

YUKO
Here.

KATE
Can't I have a beer instead?

YUKO
No.

KATE looks at the contents of the bowl.

KATE
What is it?

YUKO
Japanese stew.

KATE
Looks weird.

She eats.

That guy isn't here?

YUKO

He's visiting his dad.

KATE

The Indian.

YUKO

No.

KATE

This morning he told me he was an Indian.

YUKO

His mother was. But don't talk to him about it or he'll hate you even more.

KATE

He hates me?

YUKO

Garin hates everybody. Don't worry about it.

KATE

Why is it bad to talk to him about his mother?

YUKO

She vanished when he was a kid.

KATE

Here?

YUKO

In Vancouver.

KATE

And they never found her?

YUKO

No.

KATE

That's fucked up.

YUKO

And that's why it's better not to talk to him about it.

Pause.

KATE

Do you know the meaning of the name Pocahontas?

YUKO

No.

KATE

It means little hooker, in American Indian.

YUKO

Who told you that?

KATE

Google.

She eats.

This isn't half bad.

YUKO

Chanko-nabe. It's what sumo wrestlers have before a bout.

KATE stops eating.

Eat. There's plenty left.

KATE puts the bowl down.

What's wrong?

KATE

I really don't feel like getting fat.

YUKO

You're going to get fat anyway.

KATE

How come?

YUKO points to KATE's belly.

YUKO
Well.

KATE
I'm getting an abortion, I told you that.

YUKO
Have you found a clinic?

KATE
I haven't looked yet.

YUKO
There is no clinic.

KATE
There isn't?

YUKO
No.

KATE
So how do you get your abortions?

YUKO
There's a doctor who comes up here every three months to do plastic surgery. Sometimes, between two boob jobs, he's got time for an abortion. That's how it's done here.

KATE

Every three months?

YUKO

Yes.

KATE

And there's no clinic?

YUKO

No.

KATE

Well that's fucking stupid!

YUKO

Welcome to the Yukon, darling.

KATE

Don't call me darling.

YUKO

You could always go to Vancouver.

KATE

I don't have any money for the bus.

YUKO

I could lend you some.

Pause.

KATE
You want me to leave?

YUKO
I didn't say that.

KATE
You want me to go to Vancouver.

YUKO
If you need to get an abortion, that's pretty much your only option.

KATE
I don't want to go to Vancouver.

YUKO
Fine. Don't go.

Pause.

KATE
I could always do it with a coat hanger.

YUKO
Huh?

KATE

If I mess it up, I'll die of, like, fatal period bleeding. That'd be cool.

   Pause.

You're not saying anything.

YUKO

What do you want me to say?

KATE

You don't think I could do it?

YUKO

I think it's a really shitty idea. That's what I think.

KATE

I could do it.

YUKO

Sure. You could do it.

KATE

If you kick me out, I'll do it.

YUKO

What the hell is that supposed to be? Blackmail?

KATE

I don't care. I know I could do it.

YUKO

I told you you could stay as long as you want. So stop telling me you could give yourself an abortion with a coat hanger. It's ludicrous.

Pause.

Besides, I don't understand. How far along are you?

KATE

I don't know.

YUKO

You don't know?

KATE

I never got all that stuff about ovulations and shit. It bores me.

YUKO

But that guy from the bus. When did you sleep with him?

KATE

I don't know. A month.

YUKO

What do you mean, a month?

KATE

Because that's what I mean. A month.

YUKO

Weren't you just off the bus when I picked you up?

KATE

Yes.

   Pause.

YUKO

You were on the bus for a month?

KATE

I didn't feel like getting off.

YUKO

Holy . . .

KATE

The Greyhound buses go coast to coast. So it's easy. Once you hit the sea, you get off and you take the bus that's going the other way. If you don't get caught, you ride for free. The only shitty thing is the food. I think Greyhound has a deal with A&W. They're always stopping there to eat. Papa Burgers can get pretty expensive after a while.

   Pause.

YUKO

What are you looking for, Kate?

But Kate won't answer me
because at that precise moment
Jamie appears as stock footage in the dark of the living room.
Jamie like a gorgeous Mac truck
with his heavy-duty hands and his solar smile
Jamie, staring at, yes, her
in the back row seat of the Greyhound bus
as though there was no one around
as though the night could only serve that purpose.

JAMIE stops in front of her and stares.

JAMIE
You alone?

KATE
Yes.

JAMIE
Where you goin'?

KATE
Out west.

JAMIE
And what you gonna do, out west?

KATE
Pick cherries. Snowboard. I don't know.

JAMIE
You snowboard?

KATE
No.

    Pause.

JAMIE
I'm headin' home.

KATE
Where's that?

JAMIE
Swift Current. Near Regina.

KATE
On the one hand he seemed nice, but on the other hand there was something mean about him, you know, the kind of guy who calls you a bitch but on the other hand kisses your neck in that special way that makes you forget your own name.

JAMIE
So the power lines, you know?

KATE
Yeah?

JAMIE

Apparently, if you stay too long in a place with a lot of power lines, well, it gets into your balls and then you can't have any kids.

KATE

I can see that.

JAMIE

Worked on this site with a lot of power lines. Four hundred thousand volts.

KATE

He put his hand on my thigh, his fingernails were dirty, he was laughing really loud, not giving a shit if anyone stared at us, there was something luminous about him, about his body, as though the power lines were still running through it.

JAMIE

Know what Swift Current's slogan is?

KATE

No.

JAMIE

Swift Current: Where Life Makes Sense.

KATE

And that's where you're from?

JAMIE

Yep. So you want to put your head on my lap, or? . . .

YUKO

So how did it end?

KATE

When I woke up, Swift Current was behind us. Jamie was gone. So was my iPod.

Pause.

At one point, in the terminal, I saw a slogan in a flyer—Yukon: Larger than Life. I thought that kicked Swift Current's slogan's ass. So I bought a ticket for the northbound bus. And that's it. I got off here.

YUKO

And so what are you going to do now? You're just going to stay?

Unexpectedly, KATE turns to JAMIE and kisses him.

In order not to answer
Kate curls up in her memories of Jamie
and falls asleep
dreaming of that way he had of touching her
her body like a precious engine with complex parts
that he could assemble and pull apart all through the night.

SCENE 7: CHANKO-NABE

GARIN
And since she's here
the girl
embedded in the couch with her full belly
her itchy dress
and nowhere to go
it drags on

KATE
one week
two weeks
a month

GARIN
it drags on
she stays

YUKO
I insist that she stays

GARIN
and our lives are mixed together

YUKO
like chanko-nabe

KATE

like a Japanese stew.

YUKO, KATE, and GARIN, together or not.

Another six-pack, some pot, a disposable camera, bad pictures of deer taken in the woods out back, three feet of snow, Kraft Dinner with tuna and steak spice, the flu, a toilet that won't flush, a karaoke night, two-for-one deals on bottles of Yukon Gold, an old Alannah Myles hit, a hangover, slippers, a forty-inch TV, a rerun of a poker game, a hand cut while chopping celery, two stitches, two days off, a pickup ride in Alaska, facial hair in the sink, a tantrum, a baseball flick, chopsticks, teriyaki jerky, a picture of Pickton on the front page of the paper, four nights to beat *Resident Evil* on Xbox, nausea, the toilet that still won't flush, two hundred bucks for the plumber, three *Dragon Balls*, a load of laundry just for a pillow case, prune liquor, some pot, a glass of milk, some pot, a glass of milk, another six-pack, some pot.

YUKO

The dark nibbles away
a few more hours every day.

GARIN

The dark spreads into us
into our eyes, our skin, our bones.

KATE

The dark grants us just enough resilience
to get through the winter

YUKO
the Yukon winter

GARIN
longer
colder
darker
than life

KATE
and to believe that in the end
something is waiting for us.

SCENE 8: PICKTON PARTY

*Evening. KATE is on the couch. She is watching a newscast
about the Pickton trial on TV. GARIN comes in. He doesn't
look at her.*

KATE
Yuko isn't with you?

GARIN
She's on until nine.

GARIN goes to the fridge, opens it.

Where's that leftover steak?

KATE

I got hungry.

GARIN sighs.

It's normal, I'm pregnant.

GARIN

So then, have you figured out when you're leaving?

Pause.

KATE

Your dad called earlier.

GARIN

What did he want?

KATE

I think he was asking if you were going to drop off his cheque.
But I'm not too sure, he was talking all weird, sounded totally
drunk. Why do you have to give your dad money?

GARIN

He can't work.

KATE

How come?

GARIN

Got hurt on a construction job.

Pause.

KATE

And that money you give him . . . where's it from?

GARIN

I kill people and empty their bank accounts.

KATE

What?

GARIN

Mind you own business.

KATE looks at the TV. Pause.

KATE

(very loudly) Fucking hell.

GARIN

What's wrong?

KATE

My boobs keep getting bigger. It's super annoying.

Pause.

He would feed them to his pigs.

GARIN
I know.

KATE
They're warning people that the sausages produced in the area might contain human flesh.

GARIN
Yeah.

KATE
Sausage made from hooker flesh. Pretty sick, huh?

GARIN
Turn that down, will you?

    KATE turns the sound down.

KATE
You interested in serial killers?

GARIN
Not really.

KATE
In the ninth grade, we had to do this presentation on our hero, and I did it on Paul Bernardo. I got a hundred.

GARIN
Okay.

KATE
A lot of the time, what they have in common is a really shitty childhood. Like that they had major issues with their moms, or something. Take Paul Bernardo. So it must be the same thing for this guy Pickton. It's always the same thing. A shitty childhood and you end up a psychopath.

GARIN
Not always.

KATE
Hookers, too, that's a classic. Like Jack the Ripper. He killed hookers too.

GARIN
And why is that, do you think?

KATE
A lot of the time, the dirty side of hookers, that's part of the killer's thing. A lot of the time, he kills because he's given himself the mission of "cleansing society." A cleanup job, you know? Like, say I put myself in Pickton's shoes, well then, I tell myself that hookers are just pig food.

GARIN
That's what you tell yourself?

KATE

A lot of the time that's how killers think, yeah.

GARIN

Okay.

KATE

But you know, by the same token, this Pickton guy isn't stupid. He's super smart. That's the thing with serial killers. They're pretty sharp people. Do you know what he did to kill them, at first?

GARIN

Nope.

KATE

He would shoot windshield washer fluid into their veins. They were all junkies, so it didn't show.

GARIN

Okay.

KATE

There was this one girl who got out, right? She managed to escape from the farm with her throat and stomach slashed. Gets to the police station, all open. With her bowels all coming out of her. But she was on crack. So her complaint was thrown out.

GARIN

Okay.

KATE

So then he must've thought he had to be more careful, right?
So he started feeding them to his pigs. He always proceeded in
the same way, pretty much: shot them in the head, then went to
town with his saw. And then it was all, "Dig in, piggies! Happy
hour! All you can eat!"

GARIN grabs her by the throat.

GARIN

You want to know why Pickton killed hookers? Huh? Pickton
killed hookers because the police let him do it. That's why.
Because hookers, especially Indian hookers, don't matter to
anyone. Not even the cops.

He lets her go.

KATE

You're crazy.

GARIN

Blame it on my shitty childhood.

GARIN takes his coat and exits, slamming the door.

SCENE 9: THE RAVEN'S DANCE

POPS's place, minus POPS. On the radio, Neil Young is playing very loud. GARIN comes in.

GARIN
Pops?

Pause.

Pops?

GARIN turns the radio off. Silence.

I was waiting for you to call me back to drop by, but it was taking a while, so /

POPS comes out of the bathroom. He's half-naked, drenched in sweat, trembling heavily.

Holy fuck, Pops!

POPS
The raven came.

GARIN
What did you take, you're all /

POPS

(yelling) Look at the fire he lit in the tub! C'est lui. It's the raven.

GARIN

You're drunk?

POPS

(whispering) He's still there, see? Hiding under the couch. But he feels like dancing.

GARIN

There's no raven, Pops.

POPS

Ah, qu'il a le goût. Regarde-lé! Regarde-lé, s'il a le goût!

GARIN

What did you take?

> *Pause.*

POPS

(yelling at the couch) Sors de là, le corbeau! Viens danser! Viens!

> *GARIN rushes to the phone and dials.*

GARIN

(on the phone) Hello? Yes, it's my father. I don't know what's wrong, he's shaking, he's boiling hot, he /

POPS
(yelling) Le corbeau!

GARIN
(on the phone) What?

    YUKO enters.

YUKO
And suddenly
unexpectedly
the raven comes out from under the couch in a thunderous roar.

POPS
Le corbeau!

GARIN
(on the phone) No, it's more than that, he's seeing ravens, he's /

YUKO
The raven's body
sprouts human legs
hairy human legs with Sorel boots at the end
yet those legs dance better than all the line dancers in the world
and Pops knows it.

GARIN
(on the phone) How the hell should I know, I got here and he was
already like this, maybe he took something, he /

POPS
Danse!

YUKO
And the music starts.

GARIN
(on the phone) Three weeks, at least /

YUKO
The sound of drums
and a harp
and Neil Young, singing.

GARIN
(on the phone) I'm not sure . . .

POPS
Danse!

YUKO
And the raven dances
he dances in a flurry of fireflies and dung flies
that all hold hands to give him a halo.

GARIN
(on the phone) I don't think so.

POPS
Danse!

YUKO

And the raven is beautiful
more beautiful than God himself
for he is
God
when he dances
He is
He is Raven.

GARIN

(on the phone) Okay.

POPS

Danse!

GARIN

(on the phone) Yes, okay.

POPS

Danse!

YUKO

(moving towards the couch) But all of a sudden
right before Pops's bewildered eyes
Raven transforms
and it isn't him dancing anymore
it's Goldie
Goldie who has appeared out of nowhere
who gets up on the couch
to perform a lap dance.

POPS

What are you doing here?

GARIN

(on the phone) 14 Range Road. Bottom of the hill. That's right.

YUKO

But she won't have time to dance
the couch bursts into flames
and Goldie burns with it.
At the stake, Goldie
with Joan of Arc, the witches, a violin, and the end of love.
At the stake.

    YUKO lights a cigarette and sits on the couch.

GARIN

(on the phone) All right, thank /

POPS

(screaming) Non!

GARIN

(hanging up) What? What is it? What is it? What do you see?

POPS

She's burning! She's burning! Can't you see?

GARIN

What's burning? Who?

POPS

Goldie! Goldie brûle! C'est Goldie qui brûle dans le divan!

> *POPS collapses on his son.*

She's going to burn her beautiful body, she shouldn't have come, juste le corbeau, pas elle, pas Goldie . . .

GARIN

They're on their way, Pops. They'll be here soon. They'll be here soon.

> *They are sitting on the ground, side by side, in front of the couch. POPS is crying a little.*

YUKO

(still smoking her cigarette on the couch) But the ambulance will take
a long time to arrive
and so they'll stay there
sitting on the floor
the father leaning against the son
the son leaning against the father
watching her burn
Goldie the squaw
Goldie the mom
Goldie like a bonfire
lit from the sparks of a delirium tremens
in the cracks of the couch.

SCENE **10**: WALK ON

KATE in the mobile home.

KATE

Seven fifteen, in front of the fridge. My neck is no longer red, but Garin's fingers are still crushing my ego. Come on, Kate. Do it. Something big, something sick, something as Larger than Life as the Yukon itself. I open the hallway closet door, throw my coat on the ground, and take out the coat hanger. It's one of those coat hangers from the dry cleaners, with white paper stuck on it. I rip the white paper right off. I bend the coat hanger. I go into the bathroom. I sit on the toilet. And then I stick the coat hanger in my underwear and I lean it on the edge. Really, really on the edge; a little push and it would go in. I close my eyes. I think, I'd like them to find me lying in my own blood, the lace from my dress on the white floor, the black of my hair like a dark halo. It would be pretty. It would be so me.

She inhales deeply, as though she was going to push. But she doesn't.

I put the coat hanger in my bag like a badass lucky charm and I go out into the trailer park, among the moose antlers and the Star Choice dishes. I want to hitchhike but there's no one there. So I walk. I walk. I walk until I can't feel my legs, my face, my body, and when I've stopped feeling them, I walk on. I think, I want to become a Greyhound bus, get tattoos of dogs on my ribs, and walk in a straight line until I see the ocean. I think, I

want to get trampled by a bison herd, become a squished Mama
Burger, forgotten between two snowbanks. I think, I want to
inflate myself with landscape and explode like a birthday bal-
loon, become a rain of confetti that would snow, peaceful, in
the sharp Yukon night.

GARIN

At the same moment,
in the kitchen at the High Country Inn,
the last waitress just got turned around.
We're closing shop
finally.
No more sundaes,
no more minestrone soup,
no more turkey breast in mustard sauce.
If the clients are hungry
they can have chips,
peanuts in the shell,
or nachos, but plain, no toppings, no melted cheese.
For the first time in hours
Yuko sits down,
on the floor,
in her houndstooth pants and her dirty jacket.
She could sleep here
on the greasy tiles
between the food stains and the fries that got away.
She could close her eyes and leave,
forget about the closing procedures,
the inventory,
the clean-up.

But at that very moment she bursts through the swing doors
Kate
in her hooker lace and platform boots
stiff as a board from having walked as far as her legs would go.

> KATE *enters. Her teeth are chattering.*

YUKO
What are you doing here?

KATE
Hi.

YUKO
Did the bosses see you?

KATE
I'm cold.

YUKO
Sit down.

> *She helps her sit on the floor.*

Shit. You're frozen. Give me your hands.

> KATE *holds her hands out to her.* YUKO *puts them under
> her arms.*

What were you doing out there?

KATE
Walking.

YUKO
It's extremely dangerous!

KATE
I wanted to take the bus, but there isn't one tonight.

YUKO
What do you mean, take the bus?

KATE
I wanted to leave.

YUKO
To go where?

KATE
Vancouver.

    YUKO slaps her.

Shit.

YUKO
Don't you ever do that again. Now, come here.

    She takes off her boots.

Does it hurt?

KATE
Yes.

YUKO
That means it's starting to thaw.

> KATE *takes one of her feet and rubs it.*

Don't rub it! You shouldn't rub it. You just have to wait until it warms up. Let me.

> YUKO *takes a foot in her hands, blows on it. Pause.*

KATE
It didn't want to leave to piss you off. It was to stop pissing him off.

YUKO
Garin?

KATE
He really fucking hates me.

YUKO
I told you, he hates everybody.

KATE
He grabbed me by the throat.

YUKO
What?

KATE
He grabbed me by the throat. Look. I'm still bruised.

   She shows YUKO her neck.

YUKO
He did that?

KATE
Well I didn't do it to myself.

YUKO
Did you guys have a fight or /

KATE
He was mad because I ate the leftover steak.

YUKO
What?

KATE
It's not my fault, I'm pregnant, I'm always hungry.

YUKO
He grabbed you by the throat because you ate his steak?

KATE
Yes.

YUKO
Liar.

KATE
What?

YUKO
You're bullshitting me. I can tell.

KATE
How can you /

YUKO
Because you're just like her.

KATE
Just like who?

YUKO
(softly) Chihiro.

KATE
Who's Chiro?

YUKO
A little know-it-all who always found her way into trouble, just to prove to everyone that she didn't need anyone.

KATE
Is it, like, a manga?

YUKO
She's my sister.

KATE
Oh.

> Pause.

And your sister, she's in Tokyo?

YUKO
She's dead.

> Pause.

KATE
What happened?

YUKO
She went to a rave and was too high to realize she was thirsty. So she got dehydrated. And she died. Pretty stupid, huh?

KATE
Whoa.

YUKO
Yeah.

Pause.

KATE

So that's the real reason you came here. The real reason you were fed up with Japan. That's why.

Pause.

YUKO

Put your boots back on. We're leaving.

KATE tries to put on her boots.

KATE

It's too painful. It won't go in.

YUKO picks up KATE piggyback style. They leave.

SCENE 11: PIGGY'S PALACE

POPS is in a hospital bed. GARIN is at his side.

GARIN

How long had you been out?

POPS

Hein?

GARIN

How long had you been out of gin?

POPS

Gin doesn't have anything to do with it.

> GARIN *sighs.*

Just a small nightcap from time to time, to help me relax, that's not /

GARIN

(angry) You were fucking purple! You were purple and shaking and yelling at ravens that were dancing on the couch! So don't lie there and tell me it's just a fucking nightcap from time to time to help you relax, all right?

> *Pause.*

You want something? Like a Pepsi, or something?

POPS

I was seeing ravens?

GARIN

Yeah. Other stuff too.

POPS

Like what?

GARIN
Like stuff you don't want me to know about.

> *Pause.*

POPS
Je l'ai vue?

GARIN
Yes. You saw her.

POPS
Did I say what she was doing?

GARIN
Yes.

POPS
What was she doing?

GARIN
Ehm, nothing much . . . She was burning with the couch.

> *Pause.*

POPS
S'cuse-moi.

GARIN
No need. It's fine.

Pause.

So.

POPS
So what, Son?

GARIN
So you think about her too.

POPS
J'ai rien à te dire là-dessus.

GARIN
Just fucking please stop.

POPS
Everything I've got to say, you already know.

GARIN
All I know is that she was a Native woman, and that she disappeared when I was two. That's what you told me.

POPS
That's what I told you because that's what happened.

Pause.

GARIN

I think about her too, you know. Every time I turn on the TV, these last few months. Every time they dig up a bone or find some DNA in pig shit. I think about her.

A long pause.

I just want to know, Pops. I just want to know if she was one.

POPS
Ça sert à rien.

GARIN
What do you mean, it doesn't matter?

POPS
What does it matter that she disappeared while working the streets or while getting a pint of milk? It doesn't matter. She disappeared, Son. We lost her. That's all.

GARIN
It matters to me.

Pause.

But you don't give a shit about that, right?

GARIN takes his coat and heads for the door.

POPS

Garin.

GARIN

It's fine.

POPS

Garin!

GARIN

Don't worry, I get it.

POPS

Garin, it's not that simple, it's /

GARIN

My mother was just some dirty whore, and you don't want to tell me. It's that simple.

POPS

(yelling) Heille!

>   *GARIN stops in his tracks.*

(sustained) You never speak of her that way, Son. Never. Because I will get up from this bed with all these tubes in my arms and I will kick your ass. On se comprend-tu bien, là? You don't insult your mother. Not in front of me.

>   *A very long pause. GARIN is standing by the door, holding his coat.*

GARIN
Then tell me.

POPS *sighs. A long pause.*

POPS
I didn't do it often. I didn't go see them often. But you know,
sometimes . . . a guy's gotta do what a guy's gotta do. I mean . . .
at some point, being alone, it becomes . . . it becomes impossible,
here. There's too much space, out there. Too much emptiness, all
around, everywhere. Too much forest, wind, mountains, mud,
sky. At some point, your body has to touch someone, to remember that it is a body. If not, you become . . . rien. Nothing but a
vague dot on the Yukon map.

Pause.

The night I met her was one of those nights. One of those nights
when the Yukon is too big and it takes two to inhabit it. And it
just happened to be her who was there. At the bar. With her
fleece and her boots and her glass of 7 Up. She was there. And
I was there too. And I had just gotten paid. Pis c'est ça. That's
how it happened.

GOLDIE *sits on the edge of the bed. She's putting her clothes
back on, perhaps.*

Goldie. Is that your real name?

GOLDIE
Why do you want to know?

POPS
Just curious.

GOLDIE
You don't like it?

POPS
That's not what I said.

GOLDIE
I don't tell anyone my real name. Unless you give me your smokes.

> POPS *takes out a pack of cigarettes and throws it at her. She smiles and lights up.*

GARIN
(looking at her) So what was it, her real name?

POPS
Sheila McGinty.

GOLDIE
No one's called me that since I was fourteen years old. When I got out of residential school, I changed my name. Goldie. Prettier than Sheila McGinty.

GARIN

(to himself) Sheila McGinty . . .

GOLDIE

It's not even my real name, not really. It's not the name my mother gave me. My mother, half raven. When we got to the residential school, they gave us new names. White names. And numbers. Sheila McGinty. Seventy-two. When they sent me home, after eight years, she didn't recognize me. I didn't recognize her. And I didn't remember how to answer to the name she had given me. We just stood there, facing each other. Strangers. With no words to speak. Only silence. And shame.

She smokes.

I couldn't answer to the name she had given me. I couldn't be Sheila McGinty. So I called myself Goldie. And I left.

POPS

We saw each other a couple more times. That year, there was no winter in the Yukon. Just the midnight sun, all the way. Just Goldie, her down jacket, and the cigarette butts that piled up at the foot of the bed when I got her talking. And one day, she vanished. De même. The bartender told me she'd gone to Vancouver. And me, I didn't ask any questions.

Pause.

Three years later, the police knocked at my door. They had found you in a motel on the Eastside. This two-year-old rug rat. All alone. And on your sweater's collar it was written: "Pops: 14 Range Road, Whitehorse." So they asked me if I'd take you.

Pause.

GARIN
Why did you say yes?

POPS
I went to see you. They were keeping you in this centre with other kids. When I saw that, I thought of your mother. Elle aurait pas aimé ça. It looked like a residential school.

Pause.

This woman came in; she had you in her arms. T'étais cute. A little monkey face, with two eyes turned inwards. I'm not saying you were cross-eyed, that wasn't it, it was as if . . . as if your eyes were busy checking out what was going on inside your head. You didn't cry. You didn't look at us. You were checking out the stuff inside your head. We just stayed like that for a while, not doing anything. The woman insisted I hold you. I didn't really know how. But I took you in my arms. And then, something happened, Son. You squeezed me so tight . . . I almost suffocated you squeezed so tight. It was impossible for a two-year-old kid to squeeze so tight. Pis là, j'ai pensé . . . Your mother was there, too. Squeezing me too with all her might. We were there, the three of us, in the middle of that room. Almost like a family.

Pause.

I couldn't leave you in a residential school. I just couldn't.

GARIN
So you took me in.

POPS
C'est ça.

    Pause.

GARIN
Merci.

POPS
Y'a rien là.

YUKO
And that's when a doctor comes in
and asks to speak to Garin in private for a minute in the hallway,
it won't take very long.
And so they leave
and into the white of Garin's eyes
the doctor begins to speak.
He speaks of cirrhosis. Of an advanced stage. Of impending death.
He puts his hand of Garin's shoulder with a detatched look of understanding.
But Garin has stopped listening
because he is gone.
Horror has opened up under him like a trap door in the floor

and he falls
free falls
until he reaches a motel room in the Dowtown Eastside.

GARIN
The walls, the mattress, the window, the noise, the smells, the
noise.

YUKO
He recognizes the streets' racket
the junkies' whispers.
He recognizes the taste of fear
when his screams push it out of his mouth.

GARIN
(screaming) Mommy!

GOLDIE
You stay here, baby. You don't move.

GARIN
(crying like a baby) Mommy, Mommy, Mommy, Mommy . . .

GOLDIE
Mommy won't be gone long.

GARIN
Mommy!

POPS
You okay, Son?

GARIN
Yes.

POPS
What did the doctor say?

GOLDIE
Standing on my street corner in my down jacket. Waiting for the john, the cash, the fix. A van slows down, high beams flashing.

POPS
C'est-tu grave, ou? . . .

Pause.

GARIN
No. You'll be fine. That's what he said. Top shape, even. In a couple of days you'll be top shape. That's what he said.

POPS
Top shape?

GARIN
Yes.

Pause.

POPS

It's bad. Isn't it, Son? I'm going to die and you don't want to tell me. C'est ça?

Pause.

Son?

GOLDIE

Get in the van.

GARIN

Walk, hallway, emergency, security guard, walk.

POPS

Son, don't go!

GOLDIE

Drive a long way. Away from the Low Track, away from the city.

GARIN

Walk in the alley, over the bridge, across the Yukon, walk on the railroad tracks, walk on the main drag, walk.

GOLDIE

Snow. Wipers. Heater. "Love Lift Us Up Where We Belong" that's only coming out of my side of the speakers. Smoke a cigarette. Get to Port Coquitlam.

GARIN

Walk.

GOLDIE

A nightclub. Piggy's Palace written on a sign. Piggy's Palace.

GARIN

Walk.

GOLDIE

Slow down. Gravel road. A farm. A pig farm.

GARIN

Walk, fuck, walk!

GOLDIE

A trailer at the end of the road. Walk in the mud, get to the trailer.

GARIN

Walk!

GOLDIE

Me, getting in the trailer. The door, closing.

GARIN

Walk!

GOLDIE

The stench. The stench in the trailer. Like burnt pig.

GARIN
Walk, walk!

GOLDIE
Steps behind me. The light switched on. Me, seeing. Two purses on the table. Blood on the carpet. Blood on the walls. Blood everywhere.

GARIN
Walk, fuck, walk, get away, walk!

GOLDIE
Me, understanding.

GARIN
Walk!

GOLDIE
Me, praying.

GARIN
Walk!

GOLDIE
Like in residential school. Me, praying.

GOLDIE prays over POPS's line.

Hail Mary full of grace the Lord is with thee blessed art thou amongst women and blessed is the fruit of thy womb Jesus Holy

Mary Mother of God pray for us sinners now and at the hour of our death Amen Hail Mary full of grace . . .

POPS
There was always a drop, Son, a drop that would taste exactly like the smell of her. A drop of rare perfume, appearing in the bottle as if by magic. A golden drop in the gin, always there, faithful, like the toy in the Cracker Jack box. Every time I'd find this drop, every time I felt it run over my tongue and go down in my throat, every time, it was like believing in God.

A shot. GARIN screams.

GOLDIE
Shh. It's over, baby. It's over.

GARIN cries.

SCENE 12: AMAE

POPS
A blue gown, butt crack showing, three blood tests, green vial, yellow vial, pink vial, caw, coffee, a boring magazine, pee in a cup, run the test, dehydration, caw, normal saline, metal bars on the bed, three hard pillows, not enough blankets, the raven under the bed, tranquilizers, a liver scan, the doctor, the raven's eyes, tranquilizers, a nap, a tray with a plastic plate cover, Social Tea cookies in packs of two, red Jell-O, a bout of nausea, a blood test,

pink vial, bruises on both arms, yellow, purple, green, an MRI, the raven at the window, laughter, tranquilizers, a nap, a blood test, pink vial, a sleepless night, orange Jell-O, a bout of nausea, a vomit dish, blood, the raven soaring in the room, tranquilizers, a cloudy day, a fall on the way to the bathroom, a black nurse, a smile, a blood test, pink vial, a blood test, green vial, normal saline, tranquilizers, the raven alighting, the old woman dying in the next bed, the raven pecking at her eyes, caw, red Jell-O, caw, the raven singing, a /

> POPS *wakes up with a start in his hospital bed.* YUKO *and* KATE *are by his side.* KATE *is wearing socks, no boots.*

YUKO
It's okay, it's okay, we're here.

KATE
Not that we want to be here, but we're here.

YUKO
Well, I want to be here, and I'm here, right here, right here. It's okay.

POPS
It's okay.

YUKO
The nurse called and asked us to come. She wanted to speak to Garin, but the thing is, we . . . we don't know where he is.

POPS

Okay. It's okay. It's all okay. It's okay.

Pause.

YUKO

(indicating a plastic container she's holding) Are you hungry?

POPS

No. Thirsty.

YUKO

Anyway. I made these. They're called manjū. They're really good with tea.

POPS

Or maybe with gin, something like that.

YUKO

I don't think they serve that here.

POPS

We'll have to go get some, then.

YUKO

Ehm.

Pause.

The nurse said you weren't feeling great, so /

POPS
(to KATE) I like your costume.

YUKO
So that's it, we came over.

KATE
It's ugly without boots. But I can't put them on anymore, not since my feet froze.

POPS
I once spent Hallowe'en on a reserve. Do you know what Native folk do on Hallowe'en? They dress up so you won't recognize them and go into people's homes. They sit at the kitchen table, all dressed up, not saying a word. And they stay there until you guess who they are. And once you've guessed, they laugh, and then they leave.

Pause.

You're her sister. I can tell.

KATE gets up.

YUKO
What are you doing?

KATE
Laughing, and then leaving.

She starts to leave.

YUKO
To go where?

KATE
Bathroom! Is that okay?

She laughs. She leaves. YUKO *sighs. A long pause.*

POPS
So. Hotel pretty busy these days?

YUKO
We had a conference last week. That kept us busy.

POPS
You don't wash dishes like Garin, right? You . . .

YUKO
I'm the chef.

POPS
That's what he told me.

YUKO
I make the food.

POPS
That's it. That's what he told me. Chinese dishes only, or? . . .

YUKO
Oh no, we make all sorts of things.

POPS
All sorts of things. I see.

> *Pause.*

YUKO
Are you in pain?

POPS
I'm stuffed full of tranquilizers.

> *Pause.*

YUKO
Lucky the nurse called.

POPS
Ehm.

YUKO
If not, we wouldn't have known that you were alone here.

POPS
That's my son. Sometimes, he just needs to get out.

YUKO
Still.

POPS

It's okay, dear, it's not /

YUKO

(getting angry) In my book, you just don't do that. You just don't. Back home, you can't just disappear when someone in your family is in the hospital. It's an honour thing. If you do that, you're just . . . you're just nothing. It's so wrong that you're just nothing.

POPS

Here, it doesn't matter, dear. Nothing matters in the Yukon. *(jokingly)* Anyway, we don't need him! We can meet on our own, right?

YUKO

(forcing a smile) Yes.

    Pause.

POPS

You've been together for a while, with Garin.

YUKO

We've been living there about three years, yes.

POPS

Doing good?

YUKO

We're pretty comfortable, yes.

POPS

And are you thinking about kids soon, or /

YUKO

Huh?

POPS

You and Garin. Do you want kids?

YUKO

Garin and I are not /

POPS

All in good time, dear.

YUKO

(very uncomfortable) Okay. Sure.

POPS

He loves you very much. I don't know if he tells you, but /

YUKO

He doesn't tell me very often, no.

> *Pause.*

POPS

Go get us some gin, dear. It's time.

YUKO

I don't think I /

POPS

Go. If not, it will be too late.

Pause. KATE *comes in.* YUKO *gets up abruptly.*

YUKO

I'll be back in a bit.

KATE

Where are you going?

YUKO

To get some gin. It'll do us all good.

KATE

Wait, I'll go with /

YUKO

No. You stay here.

YUKO *takes her coat and leaves.* KATE *sits next to* POPS*'s bed.*
Pause.

KATE

Are you into serial killers?

POPS

Not really, no.

SCENE 13: LIWANU

GARIN

Long time standing.

Long time staring.

Frozen-freezing

in a shed close to the parking lot.

First, there were four,

three women, one man,

but now the man is gone

so only they are left.

The women.

Three Natives, panhandling in a group in front of the liquor store.

Couldn't say how old they are.

Forty. Twenty-three.

Dressed like it doesn't matter

half leather, half track suit

faces filled with holes and exhausted eyes.

They stay there, standing.

They tell jokes.

They bide their time.

Me

I watch them.
Their every move.
All of it.
I watch them beg.
Take a piss.
Breathe.
It's dark.
I can see them thanks to the streetlight,
but them,
no way.
I wait
stuck in Indian time
stuck in the time of the Indians
time dissolving cross-fade
time out
time limit
time powered by 220 volts of nothing.
I wait in time with all of my halves
half raven half hatred half Native half white
I wait to see which half will win.
I don't know.
Neither do they.
They don't know.
They know nothing.

    Caw.

A guy comes to buy something
one of them comes closer
asks for money

he says no
goes into the liquor store
comes out with a twelve-pack.
Another one asks him for a beer
he gives her one
he leaves.
All three of them share the beer
two gulps each and it's gone
two of them sing an Elvis tune
while the third one takes a piss behind the building.

Caw.

Later
it snows.
Later
one of them sits on the ground in the snow
in her Sorel boots.

Caw.

A white car drives by really close
he slows down
rolls down the window
one of them gets closer
but when she gets next to the car
he does a burn while honking and leaves
it was a joke
to scare them
one of them screams

one of them gives him the finger
the other does nothing
the one who had gotten close
she really got scared
so she does nothing.

    Caw.

Later
one of them sleeps, leaning up against the streetlight.

    Caw.

Later
one of them rubs her hands
another one lends her her magic gloves.

    Caw.

Later
one of them smokes a cigarette.
Later
one of them says something that looks serious.
Later
the same one cries away from the others.

    Caw.

Later
one of them drinks

a large pop from Burger King
that she found somewhere.
Later
two of them pretend to dance
they laugh.

Caw.

Later
I open my eyes.
I slept.
I think.
I slept a little.
I raise my head.
There's only one left.
Only one.
One Native woman who waits, alone, in front of the liquor store.
The other ones are gone, the other two must have left while I
was sleeping, fuck, there's only one left.
Only one.
Alone.
In a couple of minutes she'll be leaving too
it's much too dangerous to stay alone like that
panhandling in front of the liquor store.
In a couple of minutes
she'll go in somewhere.
In a couple of minutes
she'll go meet up with the others.
In.
A couple.

Of minutes.
I look at her
her
the woman
the Indian
the hooker
her
the slut, the pussy, the bitch, the squaw, the cunt, the cheap piece
of ass, the motherfucking dirty deep throat of a whore
her.
She doesn't see me.
She doesn't suspect anything.
She bides her time
alone
in the parking lot.
No one can see me.
My heart starts pounding.
My palms are sweaty.
I'm scared.
Half of me wants to
and I don't
but
this half
this half of me wants to.

    YUKO enters.

YUKO
And Garin curls up in the darkness of the shed
bringing his knees up to his belly

like when he was two years old.
He fights it
but it's stronger than him
something
has been set in motion.

GARIN

In my head I see myself walk, leave, move away from her, from her exhausted eyes, from the knife in my pocket, walk, factories, streets, alleys, walk, the main drag, the body of a dog, come on, walk, the railroad tracks, the Yukon River, walk, snow, wind, walk, whiteout, can't see, walk, finally the sky, walk, the midnight sun, finally, the night has turned inside out, walk, the sky for miles, walk, my mother's face in the moon like in the morning cartoons, walk, come on, fuck, walk, but no, no walking, but no, shed, but no, night, liquor store, street light, Native woman. But no.

YUKO

And Garin stands
and feels his way in the longest night on earth
with nothing to guide him
only a hatred born in the dawn of ages, beating in his temples
and a misty glance that splits the night in two.

GARIN

I get out of the shed. I move forward. Half of me does it. Half of me grips the knife in my pocket. I don't know what I'm about to do. But I will do it. I don't want to but I move forward. The woman's back is facing me. She stiffens. Senses me. Senses the knife in my pocket. I sense her fear make a beeline from her neck to my arm. A step. Another. And another. She's scared. I can sense it. I move forward still. She stiffens even more. She's scared of me. I'm scared of me. We're scared of me. I grip the knife in my pocket. I get closer. I'm behind her. I inhale. And I /

YUKO turns around. She is holding a bottle and a brown paper bag.

YUKO
Garin?

GARIN screams with terror. A long pause. YUKO reaches out to touch him.

GARIN
Don't touch me.

Pause.

Shit. I . . . I almost . . . I could have . . . Shit. You scared the shit out of me.

He starts to cry.

I was scared. I was so fucking scared.

YUKO
I didn't want to scare you, I thought /

GARIN
It's okay. It's going to be okay, now. It's going to be okay.

   Pause.

YUKO
I came to get you.

GARIN
How did you know I was here?

YUKO
Your dad.

GARIN
My dad?

YUKO
Your dad knew.

   A long pause.

GARIN
(indicating the gin bottle) Is that for him?

YUKO
No. In the end, it was for me.

   *YUKO opens the bottle of gin and drinks from it. She hands it
   to GARIN. He drinks.*

You can't abandon people like that, Garin.

GARIN
I know.

YUKO
No, you don't know. Because if you did, you would be there.
Not here.

Pause.

GARIN
Is he alone over there?

YUKO
Kate's with him.

GARIN
How is he?

YUKO
He's going to die. Aside from that, he's okay.

They drink.

This one time . . . I was camping with friends. In Hokkaido,
by the sea. We'd built a fire. We'd been drinking. At one point,
someone yelled out skinny dipping. So we got up, the bunch of
us, we took our clothes off, and ran into the sea. It was cold but
so fucking beautiful, the grey sea, the stars above our heads, and

the little fire on the rocky shore. For a laugh, I'd taken my phone into the water with me. Between two waves I filmed my naked friends and threatened to put it online. Everyone laughed. But at one point, my phone rang. Middle of the night. Pretty random. Everyone was surprised, everyone stopped laughing. I checked the call display. My parents. My parents were calling me at three in the morning. That wasn't normal. I knew it had to be serious. But I didn't feel like answering. I didn't want this night to end. I didn't want us to stop laughing. So I yelled, "Hey, look, a shooting star!" And I threw my phone as far as I could. It left a little white trail in the sky before it hit the water. And even though it wasn't a shooting star, I made a wish. A stupid, drunken girl's wish. When I got home, the next day, my parents were getting back from the hospital. They had tried to reach me all night. My sister had died. And I wasn't there.

She drinks.

I'm warning you. We finish this, and then we go see him. I don't give a shit that you don't want to. I don't give a shit that you're scared. I'll carry you on my back if I have to. But you're coming with me. You're not letting your father die alone. I won't let you. I won't let you regret it for the rest of your life. Shit.

YUKO *drinks.*

KATE
If Garin knew how to speak
he would tell Yuko
of the tremendous love he feels for her at this very moment.

He would tell her how he finds her strong
and beautiful
and terrifying
he would tell her that her lips shiny with gin call out to him like
a treasure
that he would like to sink his tongue between them
along with his cock
and his whole body
drink her blood and her words and carry her on his back, in turn.
But a long time will have to pass before Garin learns to say these
things.
Years will have to pass before he can speak of love.
So, for now, he says nothing.
He looks at Yuko's lips
shiny with gin like a treasure
and waits for a sign.

YUKO
He asked me if we wanted kids. Your dad. He asked me that.

She laughs. Then cries.

I'm tired.

*GARIN touches YUKO's lips. She looks at him. Then, she closes
her eyes and takes GARIN's fingers in her mouth. GARIN takes
her face in his hands and kisses her.*

KATE
And that light that you see

the green and gold glimmer that lights up the liquor store parking lot
that's not the northern lights
that's them.

SCENE 14: PROSPERITY

KATE is at POPS's bedside. She's eating the manjū.

KATE
See, me, I've thought about suicide a bunch of times, but I was never motivated enough to do it. I can't find the way, you know, the way that would mean something when people would find me. I tell myself, if you're going to do it, might as well do it in a way that's going to kick ass, a way that's going to make people understand things. Except I don't know what I'd like people to understand. I've got nothing to tell them. So I kinda feel like I'd be wasting my death, you know? I'd be worried of missing my one shot by saying nothing at all, or saying the wrong thing. Kinda like with tattoos. I'd like to have a tattoo all the way down my back, but I haven't found of what. Well, actually, I had sort of thought of this Chinese symbol, but the one I liked means "prosperity." And I don't give a shit about prosperity, I don't really even know what that means, so I don't want to have it written on my back for the rest of my life. So I just decided to forget it until I find something cool to say. Besides, I think it's really retarded to kill yourself for no reason. Or to get tattoos of cartoons and

stuff. You know, like having Hello Kitty on your back. It's just dumb. I mean, seriously, just don't get inked at all.

POPS
It means to be happy.

KATE
What does?

POPS
To be prosperous. It means to be happy.

KATE
That's what I thought. It's dumb.

    Pause.

POPS
And the kid?

KATE
What?

POPS
If you commit suicide. What's going to happen to the kid?

KATE
There is no kid. Not really.

    POPS *reaches for* KATE.

What are you doing?

POPS
I've got something for him.

Very gently, POPS puts his hand on KATE's belly.

KATE
And timidly
a name makes its way from the warmth of my belly to the edge
of my lips and escapes as a fine golden dew under the sharp
neon lights.
Prosper.
And a dark silhouette lands in a corner of the room.

POPS
The raven.

KATE
What?

POPS
He's back.

KATE
What raven? What are you talking about?

POPS
Look.

KATE

For Pops, Raven had smoothed his feathers
and put on his Sorel dress boots.

(to POPS) I'll go get the nurse, I think /

POPS

Don't go get her, dear. Stay with me.

> KATE *sits back down next to him. A very long pause.*

KATE

I don't think /

POPS

Just wait, dear.

> *Pause.*

KATE

I think I really should /

POPS

There. Look.

KATE

And all of a sudden, I see him.
In all his splendour
I see him
Raven.

(to POPS) What is it, it's /

POPS
It's for me that he comes, dear. Don't be scared.

KATE
And, gently, Raven nods slowly
and the music starts
organ music
and bells
and Neil Young singing a requiem.
And solemnly
Raven kneels
and as a cloud of blackflies recites the Lord's Prayer
she appears
her
the beautiful
Goldie.

POPS
I so wanted you to come.

KATE
I see her
with her hair of feathers and her breasts of bonfire smoke
lie down gently against Pops's body
as he smiles
like no one has ever seen him smile.

POPS

I'm so happy you came.

KATE

And Goldie's laughter splashes on the walls
and Pops's breath fades away
and for a single second
I see
their two bodies melt into gold
sparkle
and become Raven again
flying away swiftly
in the sharp Yukon night.

> *Caw. A long pause.* KATE *takes the coat hanger out of her bag
> and leaves it on* POPS's *bed.*

And when Yuko and Garin return to the room
one on top of the other
like a warrior totem full of gin and prospects
they will find nothing
and no one
only a few black feathers
a twisted coat hanger
and a window open onto our bodies' flight.

> KATE *exits, running.*

EPILOGUE

YUKO and GARIN, with a guitar. Opening bars of "Secret Tongues" by Adam Green.

GARIN

White night and dark morning
on the Klondike Highway.
A girl dressed like a doll eats a Papa Burger
in the back row seat of the Greyhound bus.
She isn't thinking.
She's vanishing across Canada.
No coat hanger.
No iPod.
While we bury our dead
in the Yukon's golden ground.

GARIN and YUKO sing.

KATE

Blossoming fireweed, a bison herd, a ketchup stain on my dress, Pepsi: Yukon's choice, back pain, a bus driver's smile, shaving your bikini area in the ladies' room at a Robin's Donuts, mountains, taiga, a flock of ravens, Garin's dad flying among them, cars crashed on the side of the road, no blood at all, garbage bags, a guy from UBC, a stuffed toy in a machine with a metal claw, an email address on a piece of paper, Mormons, stars, French fries, eighteen-wheelers, a picture of Pickton on the front page of the paper, a title in yellow, "20 more victims?," baby names, Charlie,

Devin, Sammy, Prosper, Prosper is the best one, that could be his name, yellow fields, silos, gummy bears, peanuts, mud, root beer, and the sun, the sun, finally, the sun.

GARIN and YUKO sing.

Tomorrow, Swift Current: Where Life Makes Sense.
Getting off? Maybe.
Or maybe not.

The song ends. Caw. Black.

AUTHOR'S THANKS

A big thank you to Matthew Jocelyn, without whom this adventure would not have been possible.

Thank you to Joanne Williams, Birgit Schreyer Duarte, Kim Collier, and the whole Canadian Stage team for their attentive support and warm welcome.

Thank you to Ted Witzel and to the actors and designers for the talent and love they brought to the show.

Thank you to Annie Gibson for making this publication possible.

The biggest of thanks to Nadine Desrochers, my ally, my friend, who knows better than anyone how to make my words travel from one language to another.

TRANSLATOR'S THANKS

Thank you to Matthew Jocelyn, whose vision inspired such a beautiful project, as well as to Joanne Williams and everyone at Canadian Stage whose time and care made the process so pleasant.

To Birgit Schreyer Duarte—having a dramaturg in the room is often seen as a luxury to begin with, and working alongside Birgit feels like travelling first class through the cultural journey that is translation.

Thank you to Ted Witzel and the lovely, lovely actors who made the text sing, and caw, and echo in a new land.

Thank you to Annie Gibson for engaging with this text and giving it a new life on the page, and to Blake Sproule for the careful and sensitive copy-editing that makes working with Playwrights Canada Press such a joy.

Above all, and as always, thank you to Sarah Berthiaume for trusting me with the texture of images that often, still, leave me breathless with awe.

Playwright and actress Sarah Berthiaume graduated from the Option-Théâtre du Collège Lionel-Groulx in 2007. Her first play, *Le Déluge après* (*The Flood Thereafter*), received the 2006 Prix de l'Égrégore and was read in France at the Festival d'Avignon in 2007 before being first produced by Théâtre la Rubrique, and then by Talisman Theatre in an English translation by Nadine Desrochers. Sarah's other plays include *Disparitions*, *Villes Mortes*, and *P@ndora*. Sarah has performed in the solo piece *Martine à la plage*, written for her by her artistic ally, Simon Boulerice. She is also part of the *iShow*, a collective performance piece on social media that won the Buddies in Bad Times Vanguard Award for Risk and Innovation at the SummerWorks Theatre Festival 2013, as well as the 2012-2013 Association québécoise des critiques de théâtre's award for best show.